Helen has been a Christian for much of her life. She found God's love after trauma in her life, and she and her husband were active in the churches they were a part of. Then her beloved husband died, after a long battle with cancer. Two years later, Helen herself became disabled.

This book talks about her battle trying to find her way again – hearing that divine voice of love that never left her. And her ongoing commitment to supporting her disabled son.

God's love for us never fails.

Helen Harvison

THE BRIDEGROOM AND I

AUSTIN MACAULEY PUBLISHERS
LONDON · CAMBRIDGE · NEW YORK · SHARJAH

Copyright © Helen Harvison 2025

The right of Helen Harvison to be identified as author of this work has been asserted by the author in accordance with section 77 and 78 of the Copyright, Designs and Patents Act 1988.

All rights reserved. No part of this publication may be reproduced, stored in a retrieval system, or transmitted in any form or by any means, electronic, mechanical, photocopying, recording, or otherwise, without the prior permission of the publishers.

Any person who commits any unauthorised act in relation to this publication may be liable to criminal prosecution and civil claims for damages.

A CIP catalogue record for this title is available from the British Library.

ISBN 9781398487734 (Paperback)
ISBN 9781398487741 (ePub-e-book)

www.austinmacauley.com

First Published 2025
Austin Macauley Publishers Ltd®
1 Canada Square
Canary Wharf
London
E14 5AA

Table of Contents

Prologue	7
Frozen	9
I Am Afraid	11
I Will Lead You	13
The Obstacle	15
My Promises	17
In Your Love	20
The Desire Within	23
I Choose	25
Close to Me	28
Come Run With Me	31
I Have Called You	34
You Know My Heart	37
A New Thing	40
My Answer	43
I Know	45

You Know Me	49
I See	52
My Trust Is In You	54
Come Walk With Me	57
Not Important Enough	59
Come With Me	63
You…You, Alone	66
Shine Brightly	69
By Your Spirit, I Will Live	71
Remember	74
The Long Game	78
I Am Your Way	81
By Your Grace	84
I Hear Your Cry	87
Here I Am	90
I Will	93
Yes, Lord	96
This Treasure	98
Lord, My Redeemer	100
I Am Calling	103
Come, Lord Jesus	105
Epilogue	107
Bibliography	109

Prologue

This story is an allegory – a story within a story. It draws parallels with a book in the Bible: '*The Song of Songs*', which is Solomon's (New International Version, 1984). This story maps my own life experience with Jesus, my Lord, Master, and best friend. He has been my constant companion through many journeys. He will take me on that final journey at my life's end when I graduate into His kingdom.

I started life much as the little handmaiden. I was afraid, damaged, and found it hard to trust anybody. I always felt I had to prove myself. That became difficult after I lost my husband, and was subsequently disabled. My sense of self-worth took a real dive then. I had lost the ability to prove my love to my God. I had lost the ability to prove my worth to my fellow-believers. I was lost.

Then God began to speak to me. He showed me it wasn't a matter of what I did but who I was. I was His child. And, as such, of incalculable value to Him.

We went on a long journey as He revealed this to me. And I came out the other side as a completely new person. I knew now who I was, and to whom I belonged. It didn't matter a great deal what others said. It was what He said that really mattered to me.

But apart from this, this is a story I hope for each one of us. The Shepherd of our souls extends this invitation to each person. I pray that you begin that journey, and allow Him to begin the transformative work in each life of our lives, and make us new. Above all things, this is an invitation from the Lover of our souls to take us on that journey of salvation, to set us free forever from the penalty and the power of sin. He has defeated the enemy of our souls. He overcame sin and death for our sake. So the invitation is here, to begin that journey.

And again, this is the work of the Spirit of Christ in His church, His bride. He begins that work at salvation. He completes it on His return. That time is soon. So don't delay.

When the final trumpet sounds, He will take His church home; a bride dressed and ready to meet her Husband, as paralleled in the book of Revelation, chapter 21 (NIV, 1984). This is that final journey, that final victory.

"Where, oh death, is your victory? Where, oh death, is your sting?" (1 Cor. 15:55 NIV, 1984). No. It is swallowed up in the once and for all victory of Jesus Christ our Lord.

Please read. Enjoy this tale. And enter into the joy of the little handmaiden as she is transformed by 'Grace and Glory'.

Frozen

Your heart is frozen…your spirit is like a nuclear wasteland. Your suffering…yes, it is great. I see it. You have been laid waste, as literally as a village is wiped out and all destroyed. Yes, you have suffered.

Afraid to reach out your hand, you isolate your heart, My love. You think all love is conditional because your affliction is violent. In your experience, all care is hurtful. You are afraid. Hiding, seeking shelter, and finding none.

Yet you sense something, the feeling that something beautiful is present…real, freely given…sacrificially gifted. You begin to sense My love for you.

Yes, now I am reaching out. I want to touch you, to heal you, to bring you into safety; the harbour of My love. For My love will heal you. I will clothe you in the purity of a love laid down for you, poured out to wash you clean. Yes, you know the symbols – the bread and the wine – in a system ritualistic and devoid of life. Learned by rote and punitive in nature. But in this place that you feared to be, because of the harm that you have suffered. In this place, you begin to sense the presence of a love holy, devoid of wrong intent, unconditionally given. This love surrounds, enfolds, and holds you in a warmth that is true, real, sure and that never fails. This is My love for you. Will you allow Me to heal you?

I reach for you. You are uncertain. Your past experience has taught you hurt. Yet you don't sense this in the presence you feel. It seems safe and warm. You sense good intent, a purity and truth that you had not encountered before. This intrigues you. Because of the sin you believe yourself guilty of, and the stain upon your life – you think that it can't be removed – it's there permanently. But My love is blood-given.

Yes, I died to purchase a new way for you. I traded My righteousness for your stain. I did that voluntarily, little one, because My love for you was so great.

I wanted to take your pain, the pain that paralyses you so. I wanted to take it all away. My blood washes clean. Whatever you think is there, I have taken it all away. I bore it on My cross, paying the price so you could go free. You can feel it now, feel it wash, clean, refresh, and renew. Behold, I make all things new. What is your response to Me?

I Am Afraid

Lord, I am afraid; I faint with fear. All I can see in me is unclean, unclean. I see myself as a leper in my spirit, the stain down so deep it has eaten into the bone and marrow of my life, my spirit.

Lord, I say it with such an overwhelming sense of unworthiness, "Though I wash in crystal clear water, cleanse everything about me with all the substances that are available to me, I can never be clean before You." My stain is so great, and you are so holy. Yet You say You traded Your righteousness for my stain. Can that be? Is it even possible? Your blood can wash me clean? Yet I have failed so miserably, fallen so short, I have never measured up.

But You healed the leper. And if You healed the physical leper of such an illness, I believe that You can reach down, and Your blood can wash me snow-white, brand new! Can such a wonderful thing ever be? Acceptance at last for someone like me…this is a thing great and wonderful, too great for words.

Yes, You are right. I have been sensing something, something new. There is a warmth, a presence. It's like a voice nearby calling words of comfort and peace, beckoning me out of the cold to sit by a warm fire, to be held, firm and secure. That is so much what I want, what I long for.

But I am so afraid. I am weak. I slip and fall so often that I wonder if I am really in the faith at all. I doubt…I agonise…I try so hard. My strength is futile. I am always trying, but my strength is small. I get so tired, so discouraged. I look and think to myself, that I am the very worst of all. I have tasted Your love. I have known Your strength, Your anointing. Then, I have turned and tried to follow the journey, alone…in my own strength.

And I have failed. I have fallen. I have caused harm by my words and actions. Then, and only then, I turn again and look at You. You have said so clearly that I am Your sheep, and You alone are the Great Shepherd of the sheep. You alone I am to follow, You alone I am to obey. You said *"Take My yoke upon you and learn from Me, and you will find rest for your souls. For My yoke is easy and My burden is light."* (Matthew 11:29, NIV, 1984).

You, Jesus, are the only way I should go. It is only when I look at You, putting my feet in Your footprints and my hand in Yours, that I can be victorious. You have already gone that way. It is only by looking to You, following Your example, living every day in Your strength alone, that I can have victory. I am so thankful that you showed me this.

I Will Lead You

Little one, I'm glad you have begun to understand. I have walked the path. I have won the battle. I have borne the burden for you. Just accept it at My hand. Do not look at yourself, beloved, for that way, as you have found, spells disaster.

I will lead you. I will guide you aright, little one, so don't be afraid. Reach out to Me. Reach out always, for every time, I will be there. Never did I leave you comfortless, beloved, always, I came to you. My strength will always facilitate your journey.

You have been through deep waters. You did almost drown, but at the last, you cried out to Me. Your heart is in My hands. Always you will cry out to Me. And never will I let you go.

Grief has been your portion…sorrow and loss have pursued you. Understanding and comfort have been hard to find. Those who knew you abandoned you. Confused, you drew in on yourself, drawing away from all, and everything, till it almost consumed you. But, loved one, I did not leave you there.

I drew you out of deep waters. I rescued you, because I delighted in you. Again, you made My love your portion, My strength your sufficiency. And you were not put to shame for trusting Me. I have brought you out onto a level place. I have delighted in you, and will not let you go.

Now, I'm calling you deeper. Come away with Me, My beloved. I call you to come. Will you leave everything, rise up, and follow Me?

I have promised to pasture you beside streams of living water, a fount that will not fail you. I have promised again and again, for the thirsty to come unto Me, and drink. Am I not the source from which all your yearnings will be satisfied? Did I not say that the hungry will have food indeed and that your granaries, your storehouses, will be full? Never again will there be in My kingdom one trusting Me, who will be lacking the manna from Heaven to eat. Never will there be lack, for the thirsty, weary wanderer will find sustenance indeed at My table. For the true bread, the living water, shall sustain him and refresh his soul.

Still, the question remains, My love. Will you trust Me with your whole heart and soul, finding true rest, peace at last, in Me? For I call to you now when the hour of My return is at hand. All things are reaching their apex, and time is growing short for mankind to repent.

Come to Me. Find life in Me alone. I want to be your heart's desire and fulfilment. Delight in Me, for in Me alone, you will find the life you yearn for. Honour Me with your heart, beloved. I have broken down prison walls for you. I have won the victory.

The Obstacle

Oh, my Jesus, I love what you say, I want what you say but I hesitate still because the gravity of my weakness looms up before me. To me, oh my Lord, the obstacle that this creates in my path is insurmountable. How can I talk to others about you? My sins seem too great, too great a wall for me to climb so that I can sojourn with You, with You alone, in that beautiful and far country. How I long, with all my heart and soul, to focus on You. Only on You let the world stay still. I only want You.

Is this the first step, my Lord? My heart tells me, *Yes!* and You hold my heart in Your hands. My Lord, what becomes of these shortcomings of mine? What becomes of them? Will there ever be a time when I can hold a person's gaze, not feeling that I have so much to apologise for, to be ashamed of? My sins are so great.

Lord, I realise, looking back, that over time there has been a big change in me, a big change. But there still seems to be so far to go! I get over one problem and I seem to fall into another. They just seem to multiply exponentially. Then I realise something else, there is a wonderful thing starting to happen. When I concentrate my focus on You, everything else just seems to fade into the distance. You are my priority, listening to You, spending time with You, and really getting to know You. The important thing is hearing You speak; the sound of Your soft, still voice in the quiet place becomes more prominent, and other things seem to fall into an order that suits them. These I deal with in due time. The importance is You, You alone.

But then, always, the focus shifts. I let You fade into the background and these other things take over. Then everything goes wrong…I panic…I fall. Then life is once again badly out of balance.

Help me! I want so much a steady increase in Your presence and Your anointing. I want always to come away with You, to be Your beloved.

My Promises

My dearly loved one, My precious child, I hear the cry of your heart. I hear your cry to come deeper, to linger, linger in My presence. I sense deeply your desire to come away, to be My beloved. So many, many things still hold you back.

You are beginning to be aware deep in your spirit, of the depths of My desire for you, of My keenness to fellowship deeply and wonderfully with you through My Spirit. Your past, your present, and the fears of your future still hold you back.

Beloved one, you are looking too fully at yourself. Understand this, above all things: you are a child of the King! You are a joint heir in Christ Jesus of all the promises and blessings of Heaven! Promised child, look at the promises. Are you aware of who you are? You are seated with Christ in heavenly places. You are blessed and forever blessed. You are part of a blood-bought people. You are called out in fact, and so much do I wish it were so also, in practice. You are blood-bought, a precious price paid for you; the blood of the Father's Beloved. It was not a hasty plan to bring you home, but a considered, sacrificial plan of vast love prophesied aeons of time before I, the Father's Beloved, actually came. Details were minute, but all there to the inquiring and discerning mind.

This was a purchase of love, little one, great love. You are indeed greatly loved. Respond to this love of Mine. I yearn for that time when nothing stands between us, no fear, no hesitation, but a spontaneous and unhesitating self-giving – no holding back.

So much of what troubles you is that you see the sin, the inadequacies, in you. You are still not seeing the answer, the sufficiency, in Me. You made the comment that even though you were so aware of your failure, you could see how much you had changed for the good since the beginning of your faith walk. Will you not take that further, and see how much greater the difference would be if you would keep your eyes on your victory in Me, and on My sufficiency?

You are a child of the King! You are clothed in the righteousness of Christ. You are dead to sin, a slave no longer. And your enemy is under your feet. You can do all things through Me, as I give you the strength and power. You are the Father's workmanship, created in Me for good deeds. You indeed have the victory.

Little daughter, as you grow up and become convinced of the knowledge of these truths, they will be what is impressed upon your life, not the shortcomings you presently see. As you look to Me and do not focus on yourself and the things you feel bad about, you will find a natural strengthening of the Christ life in you.

I long for, I anticipate with joy your full surrender to Me. I know that there is a time when My call to you will be answered. Without hesitation My bride will come, dressed in white, white garments, bright and clean, arrayed in beauty for her wedding. Will it be long, do you think?

How long, little one? Will your confidence in Me increase to the point that you are willing to let go of your fears, cast off all restraint and follow Me?

Come now, will you follow Me?

In Your Love

You have shown me great truths, My Lord. To learn of my great freedom in You is a truly wonderful thing. To become aware of where I stand in Your love, deeply founded on the one rock that cannot be moved, truly overwhelmed me. I am a conqueror in You. You have overcome all the power of the enemy, and nothing shall by any means hurt me. That is because You, and You alone, wear the victor's crown. You have overcome by the power of Your blood. You once and for all defeated our enemy on that cross of Calvary, stripping him of all power and crushing his head under Your feet. That is why I walk in freedom, through You and You alone.

Why oh why, Great Lord, when even as I have these truths in my heart and in my spirit, I find myself utterly shipwrecked when it comes to dealing with this world and the responsibilities I hold? Why, why is it that these truths I so delight in, I forget immediately, reacting and responding with my fleshly nature? Lord, so much harm is caused through it. So much so that I am utterly bereft and disabled through the harm that is caused. Oh, wretch that I am! What can save me from this?

Lord, it is only through Your unfailing love. You will never leave me, no, never. You will never utterly forsake me.

You will continue Your work of forming the Christ in me until I am mature and grown to full manhood in Christ Jesus. I learn again the basic precepts of, *"I have been crucified with Christ and I no longer live, but Christ lives in me."* (Gal. 2:20, NIV, 1984). Dying means pain and suffering. And this means the pain I experience as I learn, for me, it is far greater gain to put to death the flesh. For the One who was crucified for me is Lord of my whole life. I don't want the pain caused when the old nature is allowed to reign. So I will die. I will lay down my rights and strive always so that Christ's love may constrain me, and dictate my actions accordingly.

Have Your way, my Jesus. Constrain my heart and spirit with Your love, for my heart's desire is to please You. It is said that deep calls to deep at the sound of the deep waters of Your love, My Lord. And what is deepest within my heart, within my spirit, responds to the siren call of Your love. I want always to rise up and follow You. I want to turn my back on this world and live by Your truth alone. I want to turn my back on all that this world can possibly offer, my precious and only Lord. To have nothing, no one, but You, is my heart's desire.

But how do I reconcile this? Many of us have others who depend on us; family members, and many degrees of responsibility. Lord, where, oh where does this leave us? Some of us have members infirm and disabled. It would be against Your highest law for us to turn our backs on them.

You only, You only, my Lord. How? Please show me the balance. How do I learn to die daily to all the flesh wants? How do I learn as You showed me through Your trials, when all Your rights are being trampled on, to respond with love…to return kindness for evil?

I die daily. Please, please, Great Lord, let that be the state of my heart. Please let me be an example of one whom Christ has ransomed from the grave, transformed from death to life, clothed with resurrection glory for all the world to see.

Great Lord, more than anything I want this in me. I crave, no I yearn above all things, that Christ be formed in me.

Lord Jesus, show me how.

The Desire Within

Your desire shall set you among kings, among princes. Your desire, My love, is what drives you.

Have no fear. Yes, there may still be a great lack in the outworking of your life, yet your desire is wholly toward Me, to have the life of the Christ outworking in your life. Your desire is wholly to be Mine. That is the desire that drives you, gives you no rest till you find rest in Me, alone. There, you will find your peace.

Don't be afraid. Little by little – sometimes a lot – by making a deliberate choice to say "no" to a certain lifestyle, your life will be changing. Dying to self, and living to Christ, alone. This will be what characterises your life.

I see the hunger within you. I see the restless torment that gives you no peace when you are not centred on Me. To be with Me, one with Me, this is the one key that will bring you the freedom for which you long. For you become most like the ones with whom you spend most company. Being much in My presence means you become most like Me.

When I was on earth, I made disciples, those I chose to be with Me on a continual basis. These, I trained, taught, told them of the Father, lived My life and acquainted them with the standards of Heaven. These ones learned through constant association to become like Me.

You see, it is through spending much time with Me. Listen and learn. And as you learn, allow My Spirit to instil in your life the standards and precepts of the Kingdom – a life lived for, and through, Christ.

You see, it is through spending much time with Me, so listen and learn.

My desire is for you, little one. You have no need to be afraid. You must remember your security, firmly held in My hand, with the Father's hand around Mine. You are firmly held.

Remember, I will keep that which is committed unto Me. I will keep it, and never lose it.

You are precious to Me. You will be Mine on that day that I make up My jewels. You are flawless, My dove. There is no fault in you. Yield to Me. Trust in Me. If you try to do things in your own strength, it will come to nothing. But if you trust in My strength, you will have the victory.

When I ascended on high, I took captives in My train. Death and the enemy of souls are defeated foes, they can no longer do you harm. I have crushed Satan under My feet. I have taken captivity captive. I am all-powerful – the Amen – the faithful and true witness. You are safe in My hands.

By My own name have I declared, and I will do it. I will bring you through. Be not afraid, My own, My special love. In Me, you will always have the victory.

I Choose

By this time, I had become discouraged and disheartened. I had withdrawn to a place of shadows and darkness. Then I spoke from my heart, "Lord, I have been away from You for some time. I have done exactly what You told me not to: trying by my own strength to sort things out and obviously failing miserably. I have been sad and discouraged. I have been afraid to believe the true promises of my Saviour God, to take You at Your word, and to do it. I have been afraid to believe You."

You said that You would keep me safe…promising to bring me to victory, that true and victorious example of the Christ in me. I was afraid to believe Your promises.

You see, Lord, for a long time I would not let myself really believe that You had spoken to me. I told myself that I was imagining things, that I thought I was something special to believe that the God of Heaven had spoken to me. Yet over and over, Lord, I have heard You. I have heard Your sweet voice speaking to me over and over, that You had chosen me, that You loved me with everlasting love. Your love holds me securely. I am held fast in Your hand, guarded and girded by Your truth. As I trust in Your word, You lead me steadfastly, and You will never lead me astray. Your word says that I will hear a voice behind me saying, *"This is the way, walk in it."* And Lord, I do hear You like that. Over and over, I hear that voice, both with my ears and with my heart.

You've said that my heart is set upon You and that this is what drives me. I know beyond anything else in this world, or in the next, that I never want anything else outside of Your love. So if that is what drives me, then I am glad, because I know that I will complete my journey, held by Your strong right hand.

I have heard Your voice so strongly say that You have chosen me, and to do the work You have commanded me to do. When I was confused, and questioning how do I really know it's You, or am I just deluding myself…I came under direct attack by the enemy. This shook me greatly, and when I took this before You, You showed me the reasons. For I had said to You, "But Lord, the enemy of souls can not hear what is in our minds and hearts. Only You can do that." Then You showed me clearly, "Yes, My love. But he can hear My voice speak to you." And if I am questioning, ignoring, or trying to rationalise away what You are saying; then he will most certainly target me.

Lord, I don't want that. I want to walk with You, to rise up, hear Your voice, and follow You. I choose to believe that the good work You have begun in me will be brought to completion on the day of Christ Jesus. I choose to believe that You will take care of me as I walk in Your commands, meeting all my needs according to Your glorious riches in Christ Jesus. I choose to believe that what You have said, You will also do. I choose to believe that You can and will do great things in and through my life. I choose to believe that I am a beloved child of the Father and that all things work together for good for those who are called in Christ Jesus.

My Lord, You will keep me. My Lord, You have called me. My Lord, You will provide for me, You will also keep me from falling.

Your call is forever heavenward. You know my heart, dear Lord. You see Your glory enthroned there. Dear Lord, You have the right and the freedom to direct my heart however You will.

For I am Your own.

Close to Me

Beloved child, you are held in My love always, always, and I will never let you go. For the love I see enthroned within your heart is pure and undefiled. It is a thing of beauty, refined in the fires of affliction and adversity...of far more value than the riches that this world can offer.

This is what you give Me. With a conscious choice of will, refusing anything less than a full and true commitment to all that is true and beautiful, you have poured forth the fragrance of your love. And truly, it is a precious offering to Me.

Rejecting what is valued by this world, you chose to look higher. You saw the Kingdom of God, and for you, nothing less than this was acceptable. You chose Me, and you scorned the riches and pleasures of this world as far lesser value. You saw that which is eternal – an inheritance that neither spoils nor fades away. And you gave up everything else in life to attain that treasure. You chose the Christ over the transitory, and to sit at My feet was the place you chose to be. You wanted to be close to Me, near and dear to Me...always by My side. You wanted the path of the holy, above all else.

I will keep in perfect peace the one whose mind is fixed and steadfast on Me. I will never let that one fall. I will shelter you under My wings, hold you close, and carry you on the wings of an eagle to a place of rest, a mountain fortress that no enemy can or will assail. I will most assuredly keep you.

As you choose Me above all else, you will find that you are seated in heavenly places in Me, far above strife and distraction. As you learn to see yourself at My side, seated in Christ Jesus – far above all power and authority – the fear of these things fades away. They lose their hold on you. Their power to shake and disrupt your life dries up, likewise their power to influence you.

Now, this in no way means that you are not touched by the plight of men. You know that I was seen as a man of sorrows, one familiar with suffering. There were times that I wept for the sorrow of My friends. So, likewise, this will be the case for you.

Your love will be richer, stronger, fed by the Father's love, toward the sorrow and suffering of mankind. But because you have your focus on the things of heaven, immediately you will bring those things to Me. Hearing My voice, you will respond, giving My direction. You will be following a path straight, true, and without deviation. You will not be caught up or trapped in unnecessary distractions, because at all times you will be following the path of life.

Be open to My leading. Hearing the sound of My voice, you will respond like a beautiful instrument tuned to the harmony of My voice. There will be peace and joy within. I will give you light and truth to live by. And you will spurn every other way. Having tasted the heavenly gift, and proven over and over that the Lord is good, every other way will be seen as a waste, and deceitful. No. You will not choose such ways. You have truly seen these as dead inside and of no worth at all.

To hear My voice and feel My presence is what you ask for above all things. And this…this I will honour. I will honour the one who serves Me, and these longings I delight to fulfill.

Dear one, live always close to Me. Never fear to put yourself completely in My hands, because what I have promised you I will most assuredly do.

Always keep close to Me. Always, always long to be in the secret place of the Most High, abiding in the shadow of the Almighty. For there, nothing can touch you or cause you to stumble.

Come Run With Me

My Lord, I have stumbled. I have stumbled. And because of this, I have forfeited the continuous sense of Your presence with me. I know You are there, and when I reach out to You consciously, and with effort and concentration, I move closer to Your side and I once again sense You there. I once again know that I know, You are there.

But I have lost what I had. I have lost what was so very precious to me!

I sinned, Lord. You had promised to take care of me and meet my needs, asking me to trust You to do this, to take You on faith as I had so often before. You had not let me down. You gave me ample evidence that You would do what You promised, but Lord, I insisted on more! I wanted listed and documented evidence of how you were going to do that, ultimately deciding I had to take everything into my own hands and do it for You! So in doing this, I made a mess of everything.

I pulled further and further away, instead of pressing in closer against Your side. I pulled away from the presence of the saints and from worship, and Your voice became harder to hear. I began to rationalise, when with You, it's always no compromise. It started to eat away at me. I became moody, down, and tearful. Unhappy, I drew aside, avoiding others, folding inwards.

You asked me to always press in close to You. You said to me that to be in Your presence, pressed close against Your breast, was the most important thing in the world to me, and that You would honour that. To know Your voice and to feel Your presence above all things, was what I asked for, was what I seek. And that is absolutely true. And I blew it! I completely blew it. I didn't take You at Your word…trust You and obey You. I kept on asking You to prove Yourself and You already have.

You said, put Me to the test, and I will prove to you that I am true. Test Me and see. I will keep My word. And You did. And I said, prove Yourself again.

My Lord, I sinned. My Bridegroom, I have failed. You, my King, said You loved me. And I came back with "Do You? Do You?" But show me, tell me again.

You came. You lived. You gave. You suffered. You bled. You died. You triumphed. You glorified. You gifted. Again, You gave, and You gave, and You gave.

You have never stopped giving. Now, I want to stop taking – just taking. I have heard You, Lord. I do believe You. I do take You at Your word. I choose to obey You. I want to press into Your side. I want only to hear Your voice. I want to take the narrow (is it?) broad outlook that my God is in control. My God provides for me. My God leads the way. He is the One I set my course by. I am an apologist for nothing, but a champion of the faith. I will walk in His way that is unchanging.

You, I have chosen. You, I will live for. You, I will press in to know. Your voice will call me to *"Arise, come, My darling, my beautiful one, come with Me."* (Song of Solomon 2:13, NIV, 1984).

I Have Called You

I have called you. I will never stop calling you. Yes, I have bled, died risen triumphant over all of the power of the enemy. My little one, nothing shall by any means hurt you – whether angels, principalities, or powers – nothing shall by any means hurt you. I have triumphed over the enemy. I have won the victor's crown. All things are under My feet.

It is written, you are seated with Me in heavenly places. You are seated with Me. Far above all powers, My own. You are seated with Me. I have carved your name in the palm of My hands. You remember, don't you, what else is there? It's the print of the nails.

Child, I have paid the price, and victory is Mine. You are right. I have given, and given, and given again. I will never stop giving. I will never stop taking care of you.

I, the Lord, will keep you. I will keep that which is committed to Me against that day.

Draw from Me the love I am longing to give you, My beloved. Yes, press in close against My breast. You will not be disappointed for trusting Me. Keep close to Me.

I know you feel you have lost My presence. But press in close to Me, My loved one, My own, and find once again that you do see My face, hear My voice, and come follow Me.

Every step of the way, listen carefully to what I am saying. Heed My teaching, My directing, and heed not the voice of a stranger. Reach out once again. Follow the promptings of your heart always, for the heart resting in Me follows always the gentle voice of the Spirit.

Never will I lead you astray. By following closely the gentle rhythms of grace, you will find the very thing your heart is seeking, that peace that has eluded you for so long.

Remember the task I have set for you to do. This must be from now on at the forefront of your mind. Give it your strongest attention, and follow up the leads I have given you to consider, child.

I will never let you go. Your love was more precious to Me than My own life…so yes, I gave and gave, and gave again. I have given up everything for you, My beloved. And now, a life by My side is yours to be had.

Trust Me. When I speak, hear Me. When I call, answer. When I say I will take care of you, believe Me. I don't waste words. I don't speak needlessly. Every time you hear Me, it is important for you to take notice. When I check you, that means you go no further. When I say I will take care of you, I most certainly will. I will not list and detail for you all of the various ways I will do this. But at the right time, I will. Trust Me.

I carry you in My arms. I hold you close to My heart. No, beloved, you haven't blown it completely. Neither have you forfeited My presence.

But turn around when you hear a voice behind you saying, *"This is the way. Walk in it."* I will come to you. I will be there with you and I am for you. I will never leave you comfortless; I will come to you, and we will fellowship together again.

Beloved, set Me as a seal over your heart. For My love is stronger than death, My constancy, stronger than the grave. And the result of My sacrifice is a fellowship…a life with Me…going beyond the grave.

Press in close to Me, little love, and let us go, walking among the hills, drinking deep of the beauty of our love.

For this love has overcome the world!

You Know My Heart

My precious Lord, You know my heart and the desires there. You know there is within me a desperate desire for Your love to infuse every area of my life, that the gentle and steadfast rhythms of grace will dominate, and control the outcomes of my life.

Yet when I look at the outcomes, I am horrified at the shortfall I see in my life. I want to be one as separate from the world, and distant from it. Yet when I look at what I am doing…all I can see is one who is dominated by this world system.

Lord, there is little love in this world. Each person is out for themselves. All they care about, it seems, is getting whatever they can at the expense of everyone else. People of this age have sold out a life of faith for a life of self, at any cost. Christianity is seen as a dirty word. The church is torn apart, and no champions of faith stand in the gap. Any other faith is acceptable. But we are seen as those who prey upon the vulnerable. So much damage has been done by the deeds of a few. And the beautiful ones are hidden because the eyes that are blinded refuse to see the glorious beauty and the truth of Your great love.

So the old standards of faith are gone. And those who are of faith are seen as those who are deluded – as those who can't be trusted for anything.

So a life of love is needed. But my dear, sweet Lord, I find myself reacting in anger to the violent selfishness that people demonstrate against me and mine. With Paul, I can say that the good I want to do I can't, (Romans 7:24, NIV) because my sinful nature rises up and I respond before I think to do differently. Lord, my Lord, I want to be different. I want so much to have Your goodness have its way in me. So much, do I want the nature of Christ, the new man, to predominate in me. But so often, I am so lacking.

At the end of the day I sit here with You, thinking of all those times and places that I should have done differently. And I am so very discouraged.

When, oh when will I be changed to be like You? I want so much to be. I want so much to be. I do know that it's not an immediate transformation. But Lord, I feel after all this time I should be further along the road. Aren't You disappointed in me? Because I sure am. Sometimes I find it so hard to keep on going, to put one foot in front of the other, and see a new day.

You said to me that I need to place You as a seal over my heart. Is that the key, my Lord? If I place You, Your great and priceless love as a seal over my heart, I feel that might be the changing point.

Help me, oh Lord of my salvation. Help me, oh love of my heart, desire of my soul. Take everything, all that I am and will be, and turn it all anew by the power of Your love.

For Your love lifted me, turned me around. Your love set me high upon the rock, on solid ground. I know I will never be moved from trusting You. I know You never, no never, will leave me or give up on me.

My Jesus, I cleave to You in love. I will not be put to shame for trusting You. You will perform in me the perfection of Your great love, and bring it to completion at the day of Christ. You see in me only beauty, the perfection of Your love.

Step one is recognising that this world and its ideals are evil. They are controlled by the enemy. There is nothing of the beauty of the Christ there.

Step two is recognising this ugliness and its predominance in our lives.

Step three is understanding how far our natural reactions fall short of the people You redeemed us to be.

Step four is turning to You, and harnessing the power of Your love to change, to be the salt of the earth.

Step five is to be the lighthouse, the light in this dark world. And make the difference.

A New Thing

Understanding these things was a new perspective entirely. But I had to be able to put it into practice, too. I was unsure here, pondering on the "how" of it all. He opened up my understanding again, in my heart.

You are My beloved, My chosen one, the focus of My love. My purpose is to redeem, and make you 'the called out' people, to begin My exodus anew.

For it is time for you to cast aside the relics of a dead religion, to turn your back on what the world has practised, and the empty shroud of death that has been rejected by the people.

The people will be attracted by something that is vital and alive. To be on fire and filled with the Spirit is what I am asking of you.

Behold, I am doing a new thing. Now it springs forth. Do you not perceive it? I will make a highway in the wilderness, and rivers in the wastelands. Yes, I will do a 'New Thing' in My church. There will be called out people who seek the face of the Living God, and listen to His voice.

As the bridegroom calls for the bride, so I call for you. Will you come? Behold, I look for a people who will not seek the face of men, but a people who will humble themselves and pray, and seek My face, and turn from their wicked ways. Then I will hear from heaven, and forgive their sins, and heal their land.

Child, if you have heard Me, seek not the face of men but hear Me. Weigh everything. Does it match scripture? Have you risen up to follow Me? Are you wholly Mine? Seek Me, and you will find Me if you search for Me with all your heart. I will be found by you. You will not be put to shame for trusting Me.

You live in the final days of your time. There is much sin in the world, sin in the church, and many have been affected by it. So I call for a cleansing.

Let your light so shine, that mankind will see the true reflection of Christ in you, and so glorify your Father in heaven. They will be attracted to the light. And remember, that light drives out darkness.

A heart that is sanctified, set apart for Me, is a heart that is true. There is nothing false in it.

I call for a heart that is truly dedicated, and set apart for Me. I call for one so set aside, to seek the will of the Bridegroom, in the same way as a bride delights to please her husband.

You are My priority. Beloved one, am I truly, yours? Now is the time to put aside the distractions that captivate, and so easily distract you from the path I have for you.

The plans I have for you are for good, and not for evil: to give you hope, and a future.

I would use you as a great blessing for many. Tell Me…in your plans, often you have a choice that seems in itself admirable; praiseworthy. But that choice limits you to reach a few, whereas the choice I have for you would reach many. So what choice will you make?

You have before you the option of letting go of the old, the familiar, and reaching instead into a future of trusting Me completely and letting Me lead you. So will you do this?

Will you come to Me now and seek My face, turning instead to something beautiful?

Beloved, I will care for you. I will provide as you reach out in faith into Me. I will walk with you, helping you down the difficult path. I will give you the feet of a deer, and you will stand confidently on your high places.

Will you now make that adjustment? Casting out onto the waters of faith, will you accept My care, instead of insisting on the detailed plan you've relied on?

Yes, it is a walk of faith, and yes, it is risky business. But I assure you, nothing else can compensate for a life that is locked into a love walk that is through Me alone, nothing. Nothing can replace the presence of a love that has no equal in this world.

I ask for total commitment. Will you give it?

My Answer

You have called, my Lord. And here is my answer.

Yes, I turn to You with all my heart, soul, mind and strength. My desire is found in You alone. You are the most outstanding and beloved of all goals to aim for. You, I delight in You.

O Lord, I submit to You. Freely, do I give all I have and desire into Your hands. I trust You. I want nothing outside of You.

Deal with the distractions, most wonderful of friends. I want to focus on You alone. Your love is what I pursue. You are often the hound of heaven, because of the way You search out and pursue single-mindedly the weak, the lost, and those in need of Your love, until You have them all safely found, held across Your broad shoulders, and brought back to the safety of the sheepfold. You search us out, my Lord, as one searches for a hidden treasure, or precious gems. Because that is what we are to You, Lord, Your treasure, Your beloved.

And this is what I respond to. I am tired of empty, dead religion, where try as one might, one has to 'make the grade' though never good enough.

But You are, Lord. You fulfilled the law completely, and became the perfect sacrifice – the unblemished Lamb of God.

And it was all for me, Lord, all for me alone and those, like me, with a hungering heart.

Your love drove You till You had succeeded in Your task, accomplished the work of the ages. What was lost in Eden, we gained back again through You, precious Lord, that friendship and fellowship with the Master of Eternity. And now our lives are complete.

Of course, I will trust You, my Jesus. How could one resist such love? Of course, I give myself unreservedly into Your hands, trusting You for my future and my provision. Of course, I will walk with You through the night and the darkness, for You will light my way.

I choose You, my precious Saviour, far above what this world can offer. For who can light a candle to Your love? I choose commitment to the Living One, and following You to whatever end is in store for me. Because the future I have is eternity with You. And that I will not give up for anything.

I choose to be part of that 'called out' people, to have a living hope and a faith that never fades.

I choose to light the fires of sanctity, to live for a risen Lord. And I know that my paths are chosen for me, by One who holds my future in His hands.

And I will hear a voice behind me, saying, *"This is the way, walk in it."*

And, with all my heart, I will.

I Know

This began a new walk; a faith walk from first to last. All I wanted was His way in my life. The results of that were up to Him. Through seeking His face, He made this known to me.

I know and understand you, from the end, right back to your beginning. Beloved, I know your heart, My chosen one, My bride, My called out, My beloved. I know. I understand you.

I have looked deep inside your heart and seen your motivations. I know you. From your sitting down, to your rising up again, I know you. Indeed, I have counted the hairs upon your head. I know every part of you.

I understand. Each time you fall into that same trap, that same sin. For you, it's like walking into a door. That deep, violent shock of shame shudders through your body, that one more time you have let down your Lord whom you love so much…have hurt so much those whom you love.

I see it all. Sometimes you feel like giving up, you feel so discouraged. How long will you keep on hurting your loved one? How long will you keep on letting Him whom your soul loves, down?

My little child, don't you yet understand? Don't you know? You need to come aside with Me again and look deep,

deep into My love for you. I know the end from the beginning, dear child.

Don't you yet understand? I know your heart. I know it beats for Me alone. I know you would rather die than cause any more hurt to those you love. I see you – the purity of complete consecration to Me. I know.

To Me, all I want is to know that heart consecration, that fierce love that beats for Me alone, My own. And when I have that pure fire, I can burn up the old and lay down the foundation for the new in your life. I know the finished product – the Bride of Christ, dressed in white robes, adorned with the righteousness of the saints. And I see this righteousness in you.

I will have My way. When the heart rests trustfully in My love, then I am free to work in that life the transformation that faith brings.

Because it's when you know that the flesh is crucified with Christ, that you no longer live, but Christ your Lord dwells in you. You see, the transformation is by faith. Faith 'sees' what flesh and blood cannot yet see. It is heralded by faith. And reality eventually registers factually what you already knew by faith.

It means that when you really, deep down, know and understand that sinful nature no longer has the right to operate in your life. It is then that the Spirit of God is free to work in you that real change. When you are truly 'dead' to sin and 'alive to Christ', I can work in you the change that you are longing for.

Set your affections on those things above, beloved, not on earthly things which will really, not ultimately, benefit you.

'Things' will have to go. Becoming too strongly attached to those things of this life will only hurt you.

Let go of your 'rights'. And let Me do the new thing within you, that I want so much to do.

I know how it hurts you…that you draw back in dismay when you trip and fall. You become afraid to approach Me because you feel you must forfeit My presence for a time to pay for your 'crime'. This couldn't be further from the truth. For it is at that time, particularly, that you most need to press into Me, into the holy place, to let Me reach in and cauterise the pain there. I want to set you free.

Child, it is My love that will set you free. It is My love that has set you free. You see, when I died for you, I didn't die just for those sins that took place until the day of your salvation. No. I died for all sins, for all time. I gained the victor's crown, triumphing forever over sin, death, and the grave, thereby accomplishing forever what you were not able to.

My little one, I did this for you. I have already gained your victory. Will you accept it from Me? Each time you fall – and fall you will – come to Me. Bring it to Me. Let Me heal the damage done, the ravages that sin always brings. And let Me bring that change in you. You have My promise that I will transform you – from glory unto glory. But you must look to Me.

Don't look for any temporary gain that this world might offer you. Refuse to fall into that trap. Your rights and your ambitions must be given up here. Did I not show you that?

For you already know that in My eyes, the greatest among you is the one who serves, and you already know that. It's much harder to put it into practical action.

It's always a daily dying to self. Letting go of what you can get in this world, it's a constant looking away to Me, to see what I would do.

Seek the way of prayer, each time. I will give you added strength. Don't react – act in My love alone. That is what I want.

Come aside with Me frequently. Seek the place of prayer frequently. Stop, and take a moment when you are put to the test. Don't speak rashly, but speak with a considered response.

Look at Me. I will help you. You will not be ashamed. Don't be afraid. I am there for you. Always.

You Know Me

You do see deep inside of me. The very core of my being is known and understood by You. My Master, my Friend, You know and understand all of my ways. You are familiar with all of me.

My affections, my Lord, I have set upon You. I want to make You the reason I rise up, and when I sit down, when I speak and what I say. I want You to have every part of me.

You do understand my smallest, unuttered prayer, my cry for help. You know those things that shake me to my core, the deepest fears left unuttered, let alone formulated into thought. You've promised not to ever let me be pushed beyond breaking point. Always, always You will be there.

You are less than a breath away, a thought away. You see my end from my beginning. You are acquainted with all my ways. You know me fully, and thoroughly, Lord. You will never let me be ashamed for trusting You. You will never let me down.

I trust You with all that is precious to me. I trust You to keep all of that I place within Your hands. I entrust it to You. And I know that there, it is safe.

You say to come with the faith of a child. Lord, that is exactly how I come. I come with arms outstretched to worship

You, to honour You, to lift high Your glorious Name. Lord, I come with the trusting heart of a child.

That is how I give myself to You. Saviour, I give myself to You without reservation of any kind, to do with as You will. For I know that You will guard as a most precious gift the life given to You unreservedly. You will protect it as a rare and precious jewel.

I keep on forgetting that it's not just a once-in-a-lifetime thing, to take up my cross and follow You. It's a *"Take up your cross daily, and follow Me"* isn't it, Lord? It's an everyday dying to the life that the self-nature desires to live, and to choose the way of the cross instead, isn't it? Please help me to remember this, Lord. It's so easy to want to be drawn aside, to build a life on success and material values, utilising the academic gifts one has, instead of choosing to obey the voice of the Spirit of God. It's so very, very easy to be sidetracked. And many believers cannot see this. It's so easy to be confused. But listen, listen carefully to the voice of the Spirit, the life of Jesus, what are You saying to me now? What path do I choose? The way to success? Or the path of trustful obedience? What will be the choice for me?

I will always make the choice to live for You alone. I want nothing else, Lord. I hate the scalding regret of letting go of Your precious leading each day, dear Lord. I want always to live close to You, closer than a shadow. I want to be in the centre of Your love, under the shadow of Your wings constantly.

To know the sweetness of Your dear love is something so much more than anything that this world has to offer. Lord, You have asked for a love so much more than any family ties. I do understand, Lord. Loving You above all others can only increase the love we bring to our family relationships and any other relationship on this earth. It's not a blind faith. It's knowing that when I leave my loved ones in Your hands – again, with that child-like faith – I know that You are so much greater and more powerful than me, and can take far better care of them than I can. So, I leave them, in all faith, in Your hands.

You know the very hairs of my head, my precious Lord. That's a pretty wonderful knowledge to have, that You love me so intensely, dear Father. Thank You. Thank You so much for loving me so perfectly, so deeply, so very truly. You see the perfection in me. You see the finished product of me, that rare and beautiful jewel of immense worth. You have always seen the beautiful in me. Thank You so very, very much.

I See

I see the immense spiritual value within you, precious one. There is so much potential of immense beauty, deep, and productive of good and greatness.

This is what I see within you. As Father, I see within you the reflection of the Son, the Beloved from eternity, the first fruits. As Son and Bridegroom, I reach out in greatest love for the delight of My heart, whom I came to save. As the Eternal Spirit, I see the life of Christ, sometimes buried so deep. And it is this that I have come to draw out…to fashion and form into the likeness of the Crucified One who rose from death to life. This, I will always do, until eternity is gained.

I love you. I love you with the life and the power that is within Me. I desire a walk with you so close, so profound, that nevermore is there any room for anything to come between us.

I want all of you. There is no chance for such a walk, beloved, unless all your focus is on Me. Trust Me. I will never, never, let you down.

You will not be put to shame for trusting Me. I will always come through for you. Faith is trusting when you hear My voice, and in obedience, to reach out. I will always bring to pass My word to you. Don't be afraid.

You put your trust in Me more each day. You open up your heart to My love more each day. I see that trust, and My heart is stirred in response. Oh, how I love you!

You are right, little sister. It is a daily dying to the self-life, and a daily taking up your cross. It is turning My way, turning into My love, into My pierced side, where I can keep you safe from attacks of the enemy. My life is not a life easily won. It is a victor's crown won by those who turn their faces heavenwards and run the race set out for them. But neither being first nor last is important. Each person has an individual race to run, you have yours alone. And you get the prize, the crown.

My beloved, it's made up of focusing on Me. Turn your gaze away from yourself (taking up your cross) and focus all of the strength within, to Me (running to win).

There is nothing to be afraid of. All you need to remember is to keep in close union, and communion, with Me. Take My stretched-out hand, beloved, and let Me lead you, talk with you, and keep you in that perfect peace that casts out all fear. I keep you in the centre of My great love for you.

Little one, lay hold of that love for which I have laid hold of you. You are never a burden to Me, but a delight. Let Me lead you.

Many will come to try to shake your confidence, to damage your trust in Me. Do not let them, but remember that all things work together for good for you because you love Me.

Let your first response to circumstances in your life be one of trust. When you come across days that seem dark, remember that I will always be your light.

Simply trust Me in all things, little one. I mean you good, constantly. Do not give way to fear.

My Trust Is In You

My dear, my heart's delight, my precious and only Lord, my trust is in You all day long. I worship and honour You.

Yes, I trust You, my heart's delight. But still, the enemy gets inside my head, and I become anxious and fearful of the future.

I know it is wrong. But it is not unbelief that sets in. It is a more constant doubting of my value to You. I wonder, through testing time, "Do You really love me enough to take care of me?" "Are other believers more important to You?" "Do You care, really, if I go under?" so often the others don't seem to care much. And because I think that, I tend to push my faith family away, and isolate myself, too. When things get hard, I tend to feel that I'm not important enough; just a non-entity. But I know, truly, deep in my heart, that it's not how You see me.

The price You paid for me was immense. I hear You speak, so powerfully to me through Your word. I hear Your still small voice in the quiet place, over and over again. I see Your face, hear Your voice. I see Your nail-scarred hand holding mine. I know all of these things are more real than the way the world sees me. And that is what is want, what I believe.

I choose to believe in Your great love, my precious Lord. I choose to believe in a love that has pursued me and wooed and won me. You are my great God, my Redeemer, and my Saviour. Your name is Jesus.

At this time, the world is at war with those of us who love You. We are like You, derided, spat upon.

The world sees me as deluded. The world sees me as a waste of space. And I am so glad that You have called us out and won us.

Lord, I come into Your pierced side. I lean against Your breast as Your another beloved disciple. I incline my ear to listen for You. I choose for my heart to be Yours, and Yours only.

Yes, I will raise my voice in the great congregation, for You have given me a message that must be heard: a new song to sing. And that song is of praise to my King.

I will honour You in the great congregation. I will be a part of that 'called out' people, Your chosen one…Your bride.

And I wait for Your return, or that time when You will call me home. I look for You, my Lord.

Your name I will lift up before other people. Your word, and Your promises. I will put my trust in Your promises. I will put my trust all day long. In the night, I will lift my song to You. As I sleep, I know You watch by my side.

You are always here. You never leave me alone, You never forsake me, and never let me down. You always take care of me. I will lay hold of that love for which You laid hold of me.

I choose not to believe the lies of this world any more. This world system is everything I hate, everything I stand against, because it is governed by all that is wicked and contrary to You.

You are my peace, and You have broken down prison walls. You have defeated principalities and powers for my sake, for my sake.

You, I love, most precious Lord. You, I adore. You are my life, my hope, You will never let me go. I know that.

I love You, my Jesus, my Lord.

Come Walk With Me

Such great love! I felt, as the shepherdess in the Song of Solomon, (NIV), quite overwhelmed by this matchless love, He said to me.

Little one, I have said that I will always provide for you. I will keep in perfect peace the one whose mind is stayed, resting permanently, in Me.

Remember the things I have said to you in the quiet place; the things that give you joy and purpose. These things remain strong and steadfast in the hard light of day. What I have purposed, I will bring about. Never doubt that.

I bore your sins and all the burden of those on Calvary. They no longer have any right to burden you or to bind you. You are free, little one. Break forth and run freely and joyfully on the mountains of spices, on the path of My love for you. It is true, steadfast, and remains forever true. I have never, and will never, abandon you to walk the path alone. I am always there, with you.

This world system that you hate is behind you, My love. You cannot live in two worlds. Essentially, your strength will be consumed.

Live for Me. Trust only Me. You are so used to coping alone that you think that always you have to put in plans for 'just in case'. Don't! The walk of trust is to stay remarkably close to Me, with no space at all in between.

Look to Me, little one. I am the fulfilment of all your needs and desires that nothing else can satisfy.

As you walk the one path of faith and trust, the cares of the world fall away to their true place; you are free of them. Choose always to believe the voice of the one who speaks to you the peace and love you always longed for. I will never, no never, fail you.

I will hold you by My strong right hand. My strength has overcome the grave, remember that. I have borne all things for your sake. Does that not prove the love I have for you?

I will never leave you comfortless. I will keep you in that peace that is perfect, serene, and free from fear.

I will keep you from the harm of the day and the night. I will cherish you in My love that will never fail you. But beloved, keep your mind, heart and mind fixed firmly on Me.

You know how easy it is for you to be drawn aside. Don't do that anymore. It pains Me to see you so hurt, so desolate.

I have given you all the tools you need to live for Me. First, believe completely that I gave up all things to gain you. And having gained you, I hold you secure in My hand.

Believe that I speak to you in a quiet place. Who else could it be, when your heart and soul are fixed on Me?

Trust Me. Do the things I said. Walk with Me. And don't be afraid. The future I will take care of. You take care to walk closely bound to Me alone, in your everyday life.

I am always close at hand in times of need. Just reach out. I am here.

Not Important Enough

I took Him at His word, understanding His constancy with me. But once again, life interrupted in an agonising way.

Once again, here I am, Lord, Your desolate one, hurt because I was drawn aside. Lord, it pains me unbelievably to realise that it's so easy for me to get my eyes turned away from You.

It took the testimony of one I look to as a giant in the faith for me to understand what has been happening to me. You were right. I believe all Your promises, my Jesus. You said You would stand by us, and be with us, protect us and meet our needs…be our healing, our peace, to stand forever between us and the enemy. I believe that implicitly, Lord.

You said, Jesus, that I often believe that I am not important enough for that promise to be for me, too. I often doubt, not Your love, just that I don't matter enough. My King, I believe implicitly that if I were the only person in the whole wide world, You would have died for me, alone. I believe that truly. But there's this constant tug-of-war within me. I know its origin. I know that it goes back to when I was a young child, feeling unloved and not good enough. I feel always that only others deserve to see Your promises fulfilled in their lives. But not me. I don't deserve it.

But if that was to be the benchmark, no one would be qualified, would they? In my heart, I know this. There's always that "but what if?" and I am always fighting it.

I'm tired of fighting it, Lord. So tired. I am ready to accept by faith that all the promises of God are "yes" and "Amen" for me. To believe what my friend in the faith said that no matter how much I love my own family, You care so much more. You said quite openly, that which we commit unto You, You will keep against that day of Your coming. It doesn't help if we commit, take back, commit once again, and then keep on taking back. Take my family, dear Lord. Keep them, treasure them, lead them and protect them. I trust You, alone, Lord. I give them to You, and I look to You alone. I trust You. Lord, dear, dear Lord, how I love You.

My friend had said that when he was singing this particular song, You challenged him in his heart to live what he was singing. He had realised that he had become judgemental…becoming anxious about necessary costs for his ministry. Then, he realised he had taken his eyes off You, trusting You to take care of his family and ministry needs, and was at that time trying in his flesh to do the job. And that was exactly what I had done.

I had heard You emphatically promise to care for me and mine, if I would only do what You had put in my heart to do. I was so thrilled that You had spoken so clearly. I had stepped out in faith. But I had, as Paul warned us about, finished 'in the flesh', trying by my own efforts to make sure.

I was so horrified the other day when I sinned so blatantly. I couldn't get over it. I felt defeated, and unutterably unworthy. I had started by the Spirit but had let the flesh take hold. I had tried by myself to ensure, by my own efforts, my family's well-being. I had become judgemental and hateful in my thoughts where others were concerned, instead of letting Your love do the deciding for me. I had racked my brains and tried so many schemes to take care of family needs, instead of believing by faith that You would provide my needs.

I come before You, my dear One, my most precious Lord. One step at a time, I choose to walk with You. I am worthy because Your blood has washed me clean. I choose to obey You, my sweet Lord, because that is where I find peace and complete fulfilment. To stay in the centre of Your will is my ardent desire. To know the touch of Your hand, the sound of Your voice…the fulfilment that comes from gazing on Your face and hearing Your "Well done!" is my greatest desire, my heart's quest.

Here I am, Lord. I think this time I have learned to let go and to let You have Your way, to believe Your word of truth. You will take care of my family. You will meet my needs, whatever they might be. I love You, Lord. I know I am worthy because of that great love You've given me and each one of us.

I will heed You, oh Shepherd of my heart. Yours is the only voice I choose to recognise, the only one I will follow. I want only to know the peace that comes from looking away at You each day. You know my limitations. You will not let me be pushed beyond breaking point. I trust You to keep my life and those of the people I love, against Your coming, oh Lord. You will keep them and do in their hearts what pleases You.

It's so silly that when things are hardest, I shut You out. I'm most anxious and most frightened then. But instead of trusting You, I look for other solutions.

Not any more. I choose You, and only You.

In You alone, I trust. Nothing else matters in comparison with that. Lord Jesus, it is You I serve. Only You. Help me not to waver. In Your strength, I am strong.

Come With Me

Child, yes...it is so easy for the human heart to be drawn aside...so very many distractions. It is so distressing, so bitterly painful in the sufferings it brings you. These things have no future in themselves. They only serve to draw aside the ones I love so much. You, who I paid such a price for.

Do you forget so easily, dear one? Is it so far from your remembrance what I did to redeem you, the hands of the Creator nailed to that cross for you? Was it such a small price? No, you know better than that. I know your heart, child, and I know I am enthroned as King in that heart. I know your heart is not compromised, or divided. There, I am truly Lord. But you still tend to compartmentalise your life.

You feel obliged, mainly because of your background of feeling never worthy, and that you have to prove you are 'good enough'. You have this tendency to let yourself be convinced that you must prove to yourself and others your 'quality' that at last, you have made the grade! You think you still have to earn the approval. But you already have Mine. Isn't that enough? You want to be able to qualify, make the grade and prove to family and others what you can do.

Child, it seems I have to protect you from yourself. You know with what peace you walk and live when you are wholeheartedly and faithfully obeying Me. You know how happy you are letting Me have first place in all of your life. Be at peace. Do the things I have placed within you to do, and trust Me in all of this.

Be at peace. Obeying Me is not hard. In doing so, you are letting every instinct within you have its way, allowing you to go truly where your heart wants you to go. Don't be afraid.

Always, I will care for you. As you honour me, I will also honour you. I will bring into line those things in your life that at present don't line up, to bring balance and perspective.

Align your life with Me, allowing Me free reign in family, finance, activities, and interests – when you rise up, and when you lie down. Let Me be your peace, for I have broken down your prison walls.

No longer walk in suspense or concern, the feeling you've still got more to attain. You have attained life in all its glory, a life that never ends. Eternity. Paid for with the precious blood of the spotless Son of God who became sin, so that you can live. What would you trade for that? Or what could you give in exchange for that?

No earthly fee could pay the ransom price, neither could any treasure pay your life's price – it's without price. The cost of one redeemed soul is without a price on this earth.

So let's reason together, beloved. You've nothing left to achieve, for you are My beloved child, acceptable in the Beloved. Loved one, yield to Me. Let the acceptance and the perfection I see in you, become all that you're longing for. Having achieved this, you have everything you need and more left over. Let your life move at the unforced rhythms of My grace. As you grow more assured in the strength of My acceptance, you will find within yourself a different way of looking at others…through the mirror of My love for them.

You will do valiantly, tread down the naked ambition the enemy tries to bring up within you, that is opposed to My trust. Trusting means that you walk hand in hand with Me…keeping in step with My Spirit.

It is a day-by-day determination to obey the voice of the Lord and trust Him to do what He says. It means that every piece of your life overlaps till there's no compartmentalising – only a life lived in faith, a day-by-day trust that what your God says, He will do. For above all things, He is faithful.

It is impossible for your God to lie because He cannot be untrue to Himself.

So it comes down to it, little love, I want you to trust Me, but it's up to you. With all My heart, I call you.

Will you come out? Will you lay down that desire to achieve, to be recognised, to be good enough? Are you willing yet, to let go?

Oh, I can do so much more for you. Come oh, come with Me!

You...You, Alone

You are right, my precious Lord. I lay everything down and surrender completely. But then, I take back what I have given You. On Sundays, in worship, I surrender all. Again, in prayer in the evening, I confess my sins and surrender all to You. Then, in practice, I take back control, unthinkingly wresting it from You. Feeling I need to protect and defend myself and my family, I react in thought and action in ways that can in no way be considered godly.

Lord, when pain comes, I react in ways I am not proud of. When I feel vulnerable, and threatened, I often respond in ways that are not good. Yet when You were most vulnerable, You threatened not, neither did You strike back. You offered Your cheek to those who struck You, and Your face to those who plucked out Your beard. You prayed, Lord, for those who crucified You. Sometimes I wish I could warn myself that strong pain was coming, that I was going to be hurt and threatened, so I could respond in a more godly manner!

But it doesn't work like that, does it, Lord? I have to consecrate my whole life and not just that part that soars heavenward in worship. I need to have You at the forefront of my life always, every part of every day.

You are right in asserting that I compartmentalise my life. When my spirit soars in the worship of You, and I commit myself anew to You, that's how I need to be always.

I have been restless for a while now, dissatisfied. Longing, longing, to have You at the forefront of my conversation, in all of my thinking and doing every day. I want to live differently. I believe now that this is Your working in me, Lord, to be completely and utterly sold out to the Living God. That, above all things, is what I want. I know I will never be at peace until I live this way. But I have been so afraid of leaving behind vulnerable family members who I am responsible for.

But surely, I can trust You for that, my Lord? You are God over all of my life, and You love those whom I love so much more than I ever could, so surely I can trust You with them? Your word says You carry them in Your arms, close to Your heart. You're in the business of saving, and it is my responsibility to show them Christ-likeness in my living and my attitudes.

Carry them, my God. Carry them. That which I commit unto You, You will keep against that day. So I now, again, commit them to You. And my God, I commit myself to You, with all my weakness, both physical and spiritual, in the knowledge that You will keep me, You will protect me.

I can't afford to compartmentalise any longer. Take me on the journey now as I open up every part to You.

Breathe upon these dry bones, oh Lord. Raise them up to life again. Knit them together, bone to bone, with their sinews and muscles and breathe new life into them.

By Your grace, allow the life I now live to be by Your resurrection power, a life released by Your anointing to be that of the bride of the Holy One – truly radiant, truly wise, loving and faithful. Responding in love, let her be in every way the royal bride of the Most High King. I pray for Your wisdom in all I do and say. Let me conduct myself in a way that only glorifies You.

As I travel, dear Lord, mistakes will be made along the way. But I pledge to You now my oath. I am Christ's alone. In Him alone will I hope and trust. I will tremble at Your word, allowing Your Spirit free reign in every part of my life. Dear Lord, I know I will fail at times. But my whole life is concentrated on this one thing: dying to self, and living for Christ. This is my pledge.

Take me on the journey, Lord. Show me the strength of Your faithfulness. To You and for You I live.

Have Your way, alone and always.

Shine Brightly

I was exhausted in His presence, quietly lying there. Then He breathed on me.

For this, I have led you to come to this point. For this day I have eagerly waited. Little sister, at last, you have opened up the floodgates of your love to Me, and not held back the right to My Lordship over your whole life, all your being and doing.

Little sister, I am glad and so proud of you. Being in the presence of worship is your safeguard at all times. Take worship into every part of your life. This is your holiness, your life, an act of surrendering your whole life in worship at all times. Keep Me in the forefront of your mind. All your actions and your relationships will be sanctified and made holy by this attitude of mind and heart.

I am deeply conscious of the sincerity of your surrender. There was no holding back. You have immersed yourself in My presence. And all of the things you have engaged in have shown signs of that surrender.

As you walk, little one, I will keep you in mind of this. You are Mine, never more so than now, so, dear one, your walk will be different than before. You have already seen, already experienced that change. There is kindness at the forefront of all that you do, an increasing selflessness in how you relate to others. There is a conscious desire to serve the Living One, and not yourself, a desire to share His love abroad in all you do. You are never happiest unless you are sharing openly, not holding back, in the wonder of My love for you. I am so proud.

Little daughter, there is hardship ahead, and you will be hard-pressed physically and spiritually. But be of good cheer! I will never leave you nor forsake you. There are giants of wickedness in the land. But you will bring them down by declaring My victory. I have triumphed over the grave, and there is nothing that can hold Me down, no power in heaven or on earth. And that victory is yours, in My Name.

The floods will not engulf you, nor will the rivers sweep you away. I, the Lord your righteousness will protect you. When you walk through the flames, you will not feel the blaze, for I the Lord will protect you.

All of these things will come. But you will rise up in great power and know the victory, in spite of them. You will walk in My strength. Never will you be alone.

People will wonder at the victory they see in you and they will acknowledge that surely the Lord your God loves you. You will never be put to shame.

Yes, as you journey, you are learning. There will be mistakes on the way. But what you have longed for so long now will be there at the forefront of your life. Every day you will be walking with the love of the Lord your God shining like a beacon in your life for all to see.

So shine brightly, My love, My delight.

By Your Spirit, I Will Live

I will not be overwhelmed by the floods that threaten to engulf me, for You are the great rock I cling to. I will not drown in the deep waters of life that threaten to sweep me away, for Your hand, my God, holds me safe and secure. In You, You alone, do I see a total, a complete acceptance of me, as I am right now. You don't see the sins and failures that sicken me. Jesus, as far as You are concerned, they are not there. The blood that streamed down from Your hands and feet, Your head, the horror of the scourging You received, most precious Lord, to You I am without sin…washed clean, without stain.

I look and see the depths of the love in Your eyes. I have never seen such love! Unconditional. To plumb the depths would be impossible. It is vast, immeasurable. It is said Your love is relentless. It never gives up. Never. Yours is the love that searched over mountains and through valleys to find that one, tiny, lost sheep. Your love is that same love that searched for the son who had rejected Him, achingly longing for him. And when that son had at long last come to his senses, You saw him while he was still a long way off. And when he had taken his first faltering steps home, You ran and threw Your arms around him, rejoicing that You had him back safe and sound.

We tend to hide away when sin and the things of this life have wounded us, feeling we don't deserve Your closeness and Your intimacy. But that is when we most need to come close to You. That's when we need You most urgently.

So here I am, Lord, wounded and brought low by the things of this life. I come into Your majesty, Your presence, and there, I find peace. You said, *"Cast your burden on Me, for I care for you."* So here it is, Lord. I finally understand I can't carry it any longer. I really can't. So I lay it down at Your feet. And there also, Lord, I lay myself down. Here I am wounded, bleeding, sore and most sorry for myself. But purely sorry for the hurt I caused myself and others whom I love.

Lord, You know me. Precious, precious Lord, I prevaricate. I try to please everyone. And in doing so, I harm myself and get myself in a mess, largely disobeying You. So much pain, Lord. There is so, so much pain.

Lord, I come into the full light of Your countenance. I know that this is where I am safe, happy, and at peace. I surrender again to You, and Your way alone in my life. That was my undoing this time, Lord. Trying to please everyone, I did what my own common sense warned me not to. Yes, I made a commitment and pledge to You, Most High God, and I did not go back on that pledge. But in trying to address what everyone wanted, I failed to address the voice of Your Spirit within me.

I will keep uppermost in every part of my life my commitment to Christ my Saviour. I give into Your hands again my life and every part of its concerns, along with the lives of those I love. I yield these to You, loving Lord, in the knowledge that You alone are best able to take care of all of these things.

As the old hymn says, *"I surrender all to thee, my Saviour."* (Robin Mark, 2014). I am Yours, Yours alone. Yours is the voice I obey, not that of any human being…no matter how precious they are to me.

My Jesus, I have come to understand that there are things in my life that still need a resolution. You know the things that have cut deep and scarred me, most precious Saviour. There are hurts so deep that I have shut out all memories of them. Occasionally someone will say something that jolts a memory free. Then the anguish I experience and the trauma, it's so extreme as to almost completely overwhelm me. I know now that this is something I must talk with my Christian family about, and have prayer for healing, so I can go on my way, and be a productive child of God.

Meantime, I run to You for sanctuary, knowing that only in You can I ever be safe. I will keep my eyes on that beautiful face of unqualified love, drawing near to that great heart of compassion. Hearing Your voice, and obeying Your voice, Your voice only, is my safety.

And by Your Spirit, I will live.

Remember

Remember that I bore the curse for you when I hung on a tree. Remember that I have travelled the path ahead of you. Gone are the traps and the dangers, little one. Gone are the barriers between you and Me. I am always there for you. I will never leave you. I will never be apart from you. I am only a call away, only a cry of the heart. And I will come running, running to help you. I will scoop you up in My arms and carry you all your days. Be not afraid, little one, for it is your Father's good pleasure to give you the kingdom.

No human heart can comprehend what is ahead for them, that unspeakable joy ahead for them, and truly, full of glory. This treasure is yours, little love, preserved for you until that day when you claim it.

Persevere. Keep on going. You know already that the way ahead is hard, and there is testing at every turn. You know this. Remember. Your struggle is not against flesh and blood, so get your eyes off people. Your struggle is against powers, against principalities in high places. But I have defeated these same powers. Their authority against you is null and void. They give way to the Name of Jesus, and the power of that Name. And that power is yours. So use it.

See with your spiritual eyes. See the powers behind people and situations. And strip them of that power. Be totally yielded to Me. Then nothing can touch you. It's only as you falter, and for a moment take your eyes off Me. Only then can they have an effect.

But remember that now, you are called with a new name. And a new Spirit is in you. You have been washed and sanctified by the blood of Jesus and the power of the Spirit. And this power far surpasses any other power that would come against you.

You have used the power and the authority of My Name. You have seen the enemy run before you. Don't discount the power of My Name. I will always be sufficient for you. My grace will always be your sufficiency.

Remember the foundation upon which you stand, the ministry of the apostles and prophets and all who have gone before. Remember that faith is the evidence of things not seen, and being certain of what you hope for in Me.

You learn to see with the eyes of the Spirit, the things that the natural world cannot see. Be always open to Me, sensitive to the prompting of the Spirit, and My leading. I am your Shepherd, so let Me lead you, little one.

Yes, the way ahead is hard, but cast your cares upon Me, and enter into My rest. I will not forsake you, or betray your trust. That is impossible for Me to do, for I am, above all things, faithful.

I lead you in ways unknown to mortal men. But you will find all the fulfilment of your hopes and dreams in Me. Do not be afraid, little one, it is your Father's good pleasure to give you the kingdom.

Let your desire for Me be the thing that leads you, what spurs you on. Let your hopes and dreams rest in Me alone, and My faithfulness will lead you. I will be your sword and the armour in which you fight. I will go before you. I will be your rearguard. I will overshadow you. I will keep you on the way. I will be your shelter and the power in which you stand. The enemy shall flee before you, and you shall behold your victory.

Look up, dear one, for that is where your redemption comes from. Do not let this world bog you down. Always, always, I will be your hope, your comfort, your very great reward.

Find rest in Me. Keep yourself for Me, for Me alone.

I am everything that you long for. Even though I have gone away for a while, never think for a moment that I have forgotten you. My desire is for you always. Keep yourself for Me. You are My joy, My delight.

I am not looking for perfection. You still tend to see yourself as that one torn, wounded on the way, damaged goods. You must no longer see yourself this way.

I see you as unstained by the world. You are washed clean, little one, set apart, a new creation. Behold, the old has gone. The new has come. Within you, there is a fire that burns brightly, strongly, for Me. That fire will ever burn stronger. You are purified, made radiant and beautiful to Me. Unspotted by the world, you keep yourself alert to the sound of My voice calling you out. *"Come out from among them and be separate."* You have done this.

Hold hard and fast to that hope that is in you. Doing so, you grow stronger on the way.

Be My 'called out' one, ever alert to the voice of My calling. I call you now.

Come closer. Come deeper. Drink deep from rivers of living water.

I, the Lord, do call you.

The Long Game

The deeper walk was my desire. Yet life kept on intruding, to the point.

Lord, I feel overwhelmed. There is so much happening. I feel as though, at times, that I am drowning. Help me, dear Lord, oh run quickly to my aid! Draw me out of deep waters. Help me, Lord. Take away from me this burden that is too heavy for me.

Lord, I want to just draw aside and be with You the whole time, with no time or inclination for anything else. I wish I could just shut myself away from this world and its stresses and concerns, just focus on You and Your love, and what You are saying to me. That is what I have such a longing for, Lord. But this is a practice I must develop, isn't it? To be like You. You were always besieged by crowds crying out for Your attention. But You never lost sight of the long game.

You prepared Yourself. Always unfailingly, You would seek the face of the Father in between, You never neglected Your spiritual food.

That is what I do sometimes and that is where the balance is. It's seeking Your face, hearing Your voice, the touch of Your Spirit, before being immersed in the things of this life.

Trusting You that's what it all boils down to. Being obedient, set aside souls who move at the Master's touch.

That is what You were talking about. Being prepared to step out on the waters, eyes above the waves, focused on the face of the Master. As we look to You we learn to weather the storm. We learn to prove the words *"I will not be drowned. The waters will not overwhelm me."*

We run this race, and we run to win. Our prize is not some perishable trophy that spends its time gathering dust. Rather, it is one that cannot perish and fade, where moth and rust destroy, but it is imperishable, of eternal value.

Pleasing You, that is the balance. There is a song I love. The words say, "*Make me want the healer, more than the healing, the Saviour, more than the saving. Make me want the giver, more than the giving.*" Lord, this one thing I crave is to behold the King in His beauty and view a land that stretches afar.

I want You more than anything. You are my power. You are my strength. You are my enabling. I can do no good thing without You, Lord, and I want nothing apart from You. You are my desire, my hope, and I cling to Your cross. Because You are my recompense, my treasure, My very great reward.

You alone are my foundation. You alone are my joy and my delight. By my God, I can overcome an army of the enemy. I can break down prison walls. Because in You I have the victory!

You keep me close. You lead me to victory. You undergird me with the full armour of Your victory and lead me out to rout the foe. You are my victory.

You exult over me in song. You are always joyful because of me, always telling me "Well done" always saying how pleased You are, how much You love me.

Just to say that is an awesome thing to me – that the King of Heaven loves me. That One so high, powerful, mighty, would surrender His life for the love of me. This is high, beyond human comprehension. Who could attain this? But this the King of Heaven did for love of me. The lover of my soul suffered all for me and was willing to count all this cost for me.

And this is what I do for You, dear Lord. All for You. I count it all loss that I might gain You.

My Jesus.

I Am Your Way

I am your way. You turned, only to find frustration, pain and regret. Do you not yet know that away from My arms, these things will always be what awaits you?

My love for you is eternal. Now rest in that love. Know that I have loved you with everlasting love. It is something beyond your comprehension. I want you, ALL your surrender to My love, much more than you comprehend. That means that I will always seek you out. I will never leave you.

Look at Me. I will never leave you. I will always be there. Rest. Rest in My love, My beloved little one. I love you more than the heights and depths of all you can comprehend. Come, meet with Me now. I am waiting. I wait in the courtyard of your life. Always, waiting for that full surrender, letting go and launching out into the full flow of the love I have for you.

Be not afraid. I have already overcome all the power of the enemy. He is stripped of all power: an empty shell. All you hear are the dying cries. Remember.

Remember always, My beloved, in the midst of your hurt and the maelstrom of life – its damage – believe Me, it cannot have an effect if you let the fullness of My grace flow freely in your life.

All those times, all those times you've held back, not wanting to rock the boat, or cause offence – speak out.

To be truly happy, you need to lay down the burden of your old life and live My new life. Only then can you be truly happy, truly at peace.

At present, you are torn between the two. Let go of the old part of you and let Me be your every good thing.

So surrender to Me – heart, soul, spirit. Let Me be all to you, your every good thing.

Remember the veil was split in two at the time I died for you. The way is wholly open, nothing stands between you and Me. The way is wholly open. And I am that way.

Remember that, My beloved and chosen one. And remember that always in full surrender to Me, you find true peace, contentment, and fulfilment in great abundance.

Be prepared, little one. In this life, there are mountains and valleys – high peaks of glory, valleys of tears.

But let go! Don't you realise that much of the pain is that you still try so hard to do the work that I have already done? I am triumphant! Don't let the darts of the enemy find any anchor in your life. Surrender it all to Me! Let Me take that pain, as I, your Good Shepherd, shadow you through the dark night of the soul. I am always with you. My grace always flows to you, for I am triumphant.

Let your praises ring out. For I have won that victory. It rests in your hands now. So let go! Don't suffer any longer.

Walk with Me. Do not be afraid. For I will always bring you out, I will be your light in every darkness. I will walk you out there and onto the other side.

You ride on the shoulders of My victory over the grave.

So walk with Me. Do not hold back! Be everything I have redeemed you to be. Be the righteousness of God in Christ Jesus. Make the good confession before all men. Be My light and show My glory.

My strength is in you. My grace is sufficient always for you.

Now wait upon Me, as My glory fills and overflows, covering you and bringing you near. Be strengthened in the inner man. Wear that full armour of your God. Show My faithfulness that will never fail you, never forsake you.

For I am with you. Do not be overcome by fear. Fight fear with the power that you have always had, but so seldom realised.

Beloved, I am always with you. I have borne your burden. I have been wounded for your transgressions; you are set free.

I will walk with you through every fire of testing, I will hold back the torrent; it will not sweep you away.

Always, always I am here. I will not leave you comfortless. I will always come to you.

Don't be overcome with fear, but overcome fear with the truth.

My name is Jesus. Walk always in that Name. Be assured, I will keep you.

By Your Grace

The testing hurts. But I want to be the finest gold for Him. So I cried out to Him.

My Lord, by Your grace I submit to You. Your love will always win me. Without You, I have nothing. I am nothing. You, oh Lord, are my all in all.

Who am I, that the High King of Heaven would stoop down to love me? Behold, I am in reality a lowly servant girl. But Your love has stooped down and lifted me to be a princess of Heaven. In your robes, wondrous Lord, I am clothed. By Your righteousness, I am set free. You paid the price. You, and You alone did that.

It is written that my desire has set me in the royal house of my people. The '*Song of Solomon*' speaks of a lowly shepherdess, standing, keeping the flock. But Solomon saw her and recognised her great beauty. He took her and made her his beloved, setting her above her companions, in the royal court of Solomon. (Song of Solomon, 1984, NIV).

This is a beautiful picture of what You have done for me, most blessed Lord. You saw me. You loved me. You gave Your life for me. You saw in me a beauty no one else saw. You won me. Now I am seated in heavenly places in You,

Christ Jesus my Lord. I am sitting with You on Your throne, oh my God.

How is it that You could so love me? I am small and insignificant in the eyes of this world, and indeed, in my own eyes. My experience in this world is that I do not matter, my needs are of no value. I am not worthy.

But this slave, this servant girl, You saw and loved. So very much did You love me, that You poured out Your life for me and for all who would come to You. You have raised me up. I am significant. I do matter. My needs are of utmost importance to You. My value to You is beyond measure. To You, the King of all Kings, the Highness of Heaven, I have great beauty, great value, and great goodness. All because You loved me before the foundations of the world were laid. And all the attributes You see in me, are attributes I have that are from You…You alone, My God.

I look to You, my holy Bridegroom, and I cannot wait for that day when I see You face to face. I long for that day. Indeed, my spirit groans within me, in great longing for that day. The word travail isn't far wrong, is it, Lord? For it is that word that indicates the labour of childbirth. And that means pain. We suffer on this earth, as our spiritual nature groans and travails until that day when we are born anew into Your kingdom.

But meanwhile, our place is on this earth. And our job is to show the grace of Christ to the world around us. And they have to see that life.

Paul spoke of *'having this treasure in jars of clay'.* And this is true. You are always that treasure. And this body of clay is transformed because of You.

You have given us all we need to live for You. You have given us the weapons of warfare against all the power of the enemy. You have given us the tools we need. You are there, always, when this frail body is struggling with the sinful nature common to all humanity.

But that sinful nature You robbed of all its power at the cross of Calvary. You plundered the enemy. You won the victory over death and the grave. You won all power in Heaven and Earth. And belonging to You, we share that victory. I share that victory. I share that resurrection life.

Most Holy Lord, teach me to pause and turn to You when sin threatens to raise its ugly head in my life. You are all I need. In You, I have everything I need to be victorious in every situation. You are all I need. You are always with me. Teach me to pause, turn to You and cry out for Your help. You will always come to me. You have always come. You are always faithful. Your presence is real. I have seen You send demons fleeing before Your Name.

So You will not let me down now. I turn to You. I declare victory in You. Victory over sin. Victory over the flesh. Victory over all the power of the enemy. And nothing at all will by any means hurt where I stand in You, my Lord.

Above all things, You are faithful. And now, I take hold of that faithfulness, that victory.

Lord, hold me close. Saviour, oh how I need You. The longer I live, it seems, the greater my need for You.

Lead me out. Lead me in victory.

Mighty Saviour, I am Yours.

Here I am, Lord.

I Hear Your Cry

Precious child, here I am. I hear your cry. I see your heart. It gives Me great joy to hear your declaration of faith, of trust in Me. I see your desire to just be Mine, all Mine.

But as it was My decision, My journey, to face life with all of its testings, its demands, on this earth, so it is for you. It is your journey now to go ahead. You must take this trust, this surrender, and give yourself to those around you. As I did with the multitudes, so you must do for Me.

I could only find the strength to live this life by withdrawing frequently to be with the Father. In the same way that I found strength through being in His presence, so you will need to do with Me.

As you draw from Me, the wells of living water run deep. That living water is the Spirit. Through His strength, you can live this life. I will give you all you need, little sister. But you need to give out to those around you what I have given to you.

This life is so sorely needed by this world. They are truly without hope in the world. Their afflictions are many, and they have nowhere to go. It is but a little while before their hope runs out.

Will you be that light? Will you be that light in the darkness for them, as I was to the world? A city set on a hill cannot be hidden, so do not hide your light under a bushel, or behind the door, where no one can see.

I came for you to be that light.

If people, just for a moment, could see that great light living within you, they would be drawn to it, and find their hope in Me.

Remember, no time is inconvenient. When I call you, the time is always now.

Accept My calling.

Yes, I came to save you. Yes, I draw you closer because I love you so overwhelmingly.

But I love this world in the same way. So many, so many, little one, are going to a Christ-less eternity. Will you turn to them? Will you *"so let your light shine before me"* (Matthew 5:16 NIV) and so come to Me? My will is that all should be saved. But how can they, if all My people hide their light and not share it with those who need it most?

Shine your light, little sister. Draw from Me everything you need to live this life.

I know that it is hard. But this is the reason I have placed you here. Everything that you have been through, the hardships of your life, has been preparation to mould you and shape you, as a potter does the clay; to make you ready for this.

And so, I have made you ready. I have prepared you. Draw from Me. You will need My strength to fight your battles, for the way is hard, and darkness is all about you.

But remember that I will not leave you comfortless. I will always come to you to provide comfort and peace, and to strengthen you for the way ahead.

I will always be with you. I will never leave you alone.

You will endure mocking and persecution. But those who respond to the call of Christ and to the brightness of that light will be a great joy to you.

Continue on the way, little sister. It is yet a little while before I come, or you come to be with Me. Endure the time, but better still, rejoice in your place in Me. For no one can take away that joy.

So shine brightly for Me. The victory is yours, indeed. So go forth in that victory.

Will you be My vessel?

Here I Am

I will. I will be Your vessel. In all my frailty, all my shortcomings, here I am, Lord. Use me.

It's been a while, my Lord, since I've really bared my soul to You, to the clear light of Your glory, Your holiness. And it's hard, Lord. It's oh, so very, very hard.

I am no less willing. I am no less Yours. But I have been in confusion. Lord, there is sin in Your body, and it's damaging those I love. There are those who, in their pride, use what is supposed to be their gift to serve, as a weapon to control their people. You said that the greatest among us must be the slave of all. And that means a heart poured out in love to You.

And there are those who think that their 'ministry' puts them above those round about them. I know, Lord, that I shouldn't be looking at others but only to You, but it still hurts. I know the lessons You have taught me, that Your steadfast love never fails. This shall always be my song in the night, that I will see the glory of the Lord in the land of the living. The faithfulness of the Holy One shall be my joy and my song.

Man is like the grass that withers, but You endure. And so shall all of those that seek You.

We all have to learn this lesson that in the end, it's only our relationship with God that we can take with us. You are the unsearchable riches that, if a man finds, he sells all he has in order to gain it. And, again, Lord, I choose You.

At the judgement seat of Christ, all our deeds will be tested to see what can remain when tried in the fires of Your testing. And it's only those things that are done through Your love, Lord, only Your love. Nothing else can survive.

Once again, I come before You, and I bare my soul to You. I see You in Your glory. Now, there is nothing between You and me. Nothing.

I will not bow down to the gods of this world, power that mankind recognises, but which You deny. You said, *"…and a little child shall lead them."*

I am like that child, aren't I Lord? For a while, I was there. But You brought me to that place where You could speak to me, where only Your love for me was my possession. It's that love that has brought me out of darkness into Your wonderful light and out of slavery into freedom. You saved me from the terror of the night and the power of the giant. Now, I shall stand in the victory of the King above all Kings, Name above all names: Jesus.

It is a most wonderful thing, Lord. You left the ninety-nine and went searching for me, and You laid me upon Your shoulders, rejoicing! Oh Jesus, how You loved me! How You sought after me.

You have brought me through deep waters, Lord. But You held back the sea and brought me through. You were with me in the fire. And now, I have a fire within my soul, raging to be free – the fire of Your love.

Keep my gaze on You, my Lord, and I will not note the discrepancies I see but strive always to live Christ, and Him crucified – that poured out love, a sweet perfume rising before the throne of grace.

Yes. Yes, always, I will be Your vessel. Yes, always, will I serve Jesus, and Him only. As I set my course on You alone, I trust You for the outcome, Lord.

I may not see in this life what I long for toward those I love, Lord. But I know that Your love for them is again far greater than mine.

Your will is to bless, and not to curse. So I trust You with them.

As for me, I will serve the Lord. I will be Your vessel. I will bear Your love to those around me so the Name of Jesus is glorified.

Please shine in me, precious Lord.

Be my glory.

I Will

My little one, it is My joy and delight to see your heart leap at the touch of My love. The joy it gives Me is indescribable when I see you turn to the right or to the left at the sound of My voice.

I have tended your wounds, cleansing them with the oil of My healing and the new wine of the Spirit. I have taken you through deep waters, yes. And again I tell you, there is still more to come.

But I say this to you now, and most earnestly I tell you to listen. I will not leave you comfortless. I will come to you. Always, always when you call, I will answer you. You will not be put to shame for trusting Me.

Though the answer is delayed, wait for it. It will surely come. You will never be alone again.

The waters may threaten to sweep you away, little sister. But I will be there with you holding them back. When the waves are highest, that's when you must most earnestly look to Me. I will keep you. I will comfort you. I will not forsake you.

Be patient within the fires of affliction, beloved one. For those fires burn out only what is not perfect in My sight. They can never threaten the beautiful jewel being forged within, that the kings of this earth would marvel at, so rare is its beauty. Look to Me, little love. For I am right there by your side. When you walk through the fire, you will not be burned; the flames will not set you ablaze.

Trust Me. You will never be put to shame for doing so. Walk in My love. Give no foothold to the flesh.

As you increase your gaze into My face, so also the things of this world will fade away. Give way, little love. It doesn't hurt you to do so. Remember that the mind set on the Spirit gives the greatest priority to Me and My calling.

Now look to Me. Yes, I have taken you so very far. But still, the journey continues on. So far you've come, but still, there is so far to go. Do you know, the hardest battles are just in the day-to-day of your daily existence?

Great love you do have! Great faith to do exploits! But I ask you to focus on the every day and complete the task I ask of you.

Run your race now! Strain with every fibre of your being, giving your all for your King. Live the life, little one. Move at the unforced rhythms of My grace, and I will surely bless you.

Live for Me. Trust Me for the outcomes as you obey, using what I have given you in the full armour of grace. And having done all, stand! Stand your ground! Don't give way to the attacks of the enemy and don't be unaware of his treachery. He will take what is good and turn it into evil.

Stand your ground! Stand, knowing that the Lord of Hosts is your rearguard, nothing shall by any means hurt you.

Look to Me, little sister. Then, you will find that what seemed so large pales to insignificance in the light of My love for you.

Be not afraid, little flock, for it is your Father's good pleasure to give you the kingdom (Luke 12:31, NIV, 1984).

Be of good cheer.

Yes, Lord

Yes, Lord. I respond gladly to the sound of Your voice, to the joy of Your direction. I draw strength from Your presence, Lord. You stand by me in the quiet times, when I draw aside with You. I can truly say that My God walks with me. Yes, He talks with me as a man talks with his friend.

To be the friend of God, what a glorious privilege. Most certainly a privilege one would trade all the treasures of the world for. To be the Lord's beloved? What joy dwells in this phrase! To put into words the glory of this position, the most unspeakable joy this entails, where would one start?

I see myself as a queen, the bride of the Most High. I am seated in Heaven, the utmost beauty of that place. All is imbued with a pure, shining brightness that it would be impossible to paint, as it is layer upon layer, immense depths and multi-dimensional. Time is at an end. Grace has triumphed. The stain of sin is defeated. That is why there is this multi-layered glorious light, complete purity.

The Son in His glory is enthroned in majesty at its preeminence! His glory blazes forth, His bride takes her place at His side, and the saints of the ages who have triumphed by the blood of the Lamb and by the word of their testimony. She has washed her robes, making them white by His blood. It is a scene of great victory and rejoicing: the saints singing His praises and the angelic host exulting in loud and mighty praises. How wonderful it is! But the battle is won as by faith we take His hand and learn to walk on the waters of life. And I know I can do this.

Lord, in You I am a conqueror. By Your Name I can stand before giants of fear and intimidation, declaring victory in Jesus' Name.

You have promised me that I shall not be overwhelmed. Lord, it's so hard right now but I know that one step at a time, I can overcome. Lord, You don't ask me to see the big picture and all in one fell swoop be able to deal with it. No, it's day by day, a little at a time. Trusting You for the next step, it's one day at a time, step by step and page by page of the story.

It's learning to not have to be in total control, but surrendering control to You. It's allowing You to – day by day, step by step, page by page – put into our hearts what You want us to do. Trusting You, then, to supply us with the means to do it.

You will never let me down. You will never leave me alone. I am Your well-loved one, chosen and precious in Your sight. You are the chief cornerstone on which I build my life.

You were right when You said it would get harder. It has, Lord. But as You always do, You provide a way out so I can bear up under it. You are Way-Maker. I trust You to always make that way.

I walk on the waters, dear Lord, eyes firmly fixed on You.

Sometimes I might waver, but I will never fall. For I am founded on the rock.

This Treasure

I see your faith, dear one. I see clearly the faithfulness in your heart – the pure steadfastness that trusts utterly; the trust born in the fires of affliction. Those tested, have had their trust purified and refined. It is truly the treasure of heaven.

For this treasure isn't simply the rare stones of great value that the world runs after. No, this treasure could not be bought with everything that the world could offer up. This treasure finds its way to the Father's heart. This treasure was that *'pearl of great price'* (Matt. 13:45, NIV, 1984), that I offered up My life to gain.

Precious one, behold, I have sought you and I have found you. I could see in you a beauty that doesn't belong here, something that the world looks at, then shakes its head in total incomprehension. For, dear one, what I see deep down in your heart, is a yearning for a love that is faithful, true, and steadfast. This love that I have for you will last the test of time. I am always here. Never will I abandon you.

That is why you run and hide sometimes. You feel that you've missed the mark. Surely, oh surely, your heart says to you that He cannot love me now.

But, little one, My love for you will continue on. It shall not fail you.

I know your heart better than you know it yourself. I know the pain. I see the ongoing pressure to care, to keep on caring even when you're struggling, overwhelmed with exhaustion, the physical pressure building up to the extent that you wonder how long you can keep on going.

Dear one, it is My desire to carry you at these times. But come to Me, turn to Me, and surrender the burden. I will carry you in My arms, hold you close to My heart. You shall find rest.

Little one, there will never come a time when I will turn away from you. I am faithful, utterly faithful.

Time and time again you've been let down in the past – betrayed. You see My heart, as I see yours, dear one. Behold, My love for you led Me to a cross of shame where all your inadequacies were laid down and dealt with, your failures and shame exchanged for My righteousness.

Never will I leave you. Never. I have carved your name in the hollows of My hands. There is a place for you to burrow into My side and find comfort there.

Oh, I see your heart and I rejoice that you are one who sees clearly now, eyes not blinded by the lies of the deceiver. My heart, My love is a constant in your life. I am always by your side. You, little one, have been lifted up into heavenly places at the side of your Redeemer. Not far to go now. Your battle is almost done; your race is run. Never be afraid again. For your Redeemer is strong. The Lord of Hosts is His name.

But press on just a little longer…just a little longer.

Soon…soon you will see Me.

So be strong. Be comforted. You are Mine. Do not be afraid. I will never, no, never leave you alone.

Soon, I will come to you.

Lord, My Redeemer

You hold that title, my Redeemer, the name above every other, the name of Jesus. At Your name demons bow, those captives are set free, their blind eyes open, and sins are forgiven. New life comes to those living in You. The hope of the hopeless, You become their hope and new life begins.

I have given my life to You and You have taken me on a journey. I am loved with everlasting love and one that will never fail. You never let me down. Because I love You more than life itself, You have lifted me up to heavenly places, and I have become a child of the King. Your rule is a rule that will never end. You have triumphed over sin and death. And soon, You will come again and take me to Yourself, so that where You are, I can also be. This gives me great joy, my Lord. So here I am again to bow down before You and cry 'Holy' for holy, You are.

Jesus, Your love covers a multitude of sins…Your shed blood has washed clean my life, and all the lives of those who live trusting You and live to be with You.

My dear and most glorious Lord, I worship You. You have broken the chains of slavery to sin. You have set me free.

You suffered. Because of the great love You have for me, You bore the uncleanness of my shame. You have set me free.

And because of that freedom, I am free, every day, to choose to trust You, and to choose Your way. What You have said, You will do. I have proven that over and over again. You are always faithful.

I am free to be Yours. I can see clearly now. There is no other life I care for. You are my hope. I live to serve You, to only be Yours.

It's like in a marriage, only much closer. Down through the ages, and still, in other cultures, the groom-to-be had to pay the bride price. And Lord, the price You had to pay was the highest since the beginning of time, and for eternity past. For the price You paid to call me Your own was Your blood, for as it is written, *"Without the shedding of blood, there is no forgiveness."*

You loved me so very, very much that You couldn't bear to see me enslaved by such a cruel task-master. So You suffered, You died, but You triumphed because it was impossible for death to hold You.

So You have that Name that is above every name, that at the name of Jesus every knee shall bow, in heaven above, on earth, and under the earth. And every tongue confesses that He is Lord, to the glory of God the Father.

Your Father must be so proud of You. I call Him 'Abba' too, Lord, because of You.

I just want each day, to be Your beloved…to hear Your voice calling to me in the watches of the night…to hear You whisper Your love to me in the soft touches of the morning breeze. To come aside when You call me, Lord, for it is always something new for my, or for another's journey.

Lord, I look to that day. I look to that day of days above all things when You call me home and say, "Well done, beloved! Welcome home!"

I Am Calling

I am so glad, so very, very glad. The eyes of your heart have been opened to see the truth. My love for you, My beloved, knows no bounds. Abba, Father…He is your Father and Mine. A place is prepared for you at My table, on that day when I catch you away, calling you home. I look forward to that day when face to face at last, we will be…with nothing in between.

No barriers now. No holding back. I joy over with you with such singing, such glad rejoicing, that on that day you will hear for yourself.

At the marriage supper of the Lamb, all will be welcome who have chosen to name Me as Lord. You are of that number. You have chosen Me, as in ages past before the creation of the world, I chose you as My own. I could see, even then, the response of a heart tried, tested, and true. You would come to Me seeking safety in My loving arms. I joy over you, My most precious child. I exult in My love for you, and yours for Me. I rejoice in the closeness we enjoy in our walk together increasingly, as the eyes of your heart are opened, you see clearly, openly, My love, as I guide you home.

Now is the time I am calling you. Lay aside all those burdens that are the things of this life. Lay those burdens down, little sister. Know in your heart as the truth of My love and faithfulness grow stronger in you, that there is no way I can ever let you down. Declare My love for you. Declare it with all the conviction of your spirit, knowing in the farthest reaches of your spirit the veracity of this statement.

I love you. I have called you. I have led you through some pretty deep waters, yet here you are, safe, intact, and stronger from the experiences. The fires of affliction have burned with an intense heat. But there, I was with you.

I shall never fail you. My love will last an eternity. I have all that time to tell you in great detail how much you mean to Me, how great is the beauty I see in you.

Don't be afraid. Those you love will always be cared for, more infinitely again than it is within your power to do. When I call you away to that walk that continues on the other side, there will be those to take up that mantle of care you have worn for so long. And as those loved by you turn to Me, again, I will prove faithful. I will lead them through, like you, to that inheritance that never fades, where they, too, can cry 'Abba, Father'.

So don't be afraid, child of My love. It is nearly time. That moment is almost here when I will cry "Come away, My beloved!" and will call you home. There, you shall see Me.

Come, Lord Jesus

Even so, "Come, Lord Jesus." This is the cry of my heart now, and forever.

And so, the journeys of the little handmaiden ended. Her Lord had called her home.

This story is an allegory. It typifies what the Song of Songs, called Solomon's, is often interpreted as the intimate and intense love God has for His people. So it is with this story.

Each one of us, irrespective of whether we are male or female, makes up the church, which is the Bride of Christ. He is calling you and me into that faith walk, as the Shepherd called the little handmaiden, deeper and deeper into complete reliance on Him and surrender to Him. This is what He wants for you and for me.

He doesn't see us as other people do. They see the outside. So, also (and I say this to our shame) do much of the church. Others see age, disability, and restrictions in the natural that affect our daily lives. Our wonderful Saviour sees deeper, oh, so much deeper!

He sees the searing white pure love of a heart sold out to Him alone. He doesn't see the natural, only our surrender to

Him. He can do, oh, so very much, with a heart that's available, a life lived moment by moment, for Him.

So I invite you on a journey. Other people call it life. It is a life that I have learned and I am learning to yield, by trusting Him. It is a life in which I am learning, that He is always, utterly, faithful.

Will you come with me? Will you join me on a journey that daily opens up to new revelations of the wonder-working God to whom we belong?

He is faithful. That is His name. And I look forward to that day to come when His bride, dressed in fine linen, white and clean, will walk clear into Heaven with that *"Well done, My good and faithful servant! Enter into the joy of your Lord!"*

Maranatha! Even so, come, Lord Jesus.

Epilogue

And so, the journeys of the little handmaiden had ended. She had gone home with her Lord, the lover of her soul.

She hadn't realised, in the journey, that she had become transformed. She had changed from one who was much-fearing, battling with life on every level, to one who was 'Glory and Grace' that was the name she had been given. Her Lord had transformed her.

You see, the secret here was focusing on her Lord, and not on her problems. That had given Him all that was necessary to work His transforming power within her. She no longer feared, she trusted. She knew that whatever this life threw at her, His love and grace would get her through.

This doesn't mean that it became easy for her. No, in many ways, it was harder. For the enemy of our souls doesn't like his reign to be disputed. And the moment we put Jesus at the forefront of our lives, we do just that.

The secret is making Jesus Christ the Lord of our lives. That way, He can begin His transformative work within our lives. He literally makes us those beings of 'Grace and Glory', our lives founded on the true foundation stone upon which God's whole church is built. And nothing can shake that foundation.

So will you join me on this incredible journey? It is amazing and mind-blowing in many ways. But oh, so worth it! Let Jesus be Lord. And join me on the journey of *'The Bridegroom and I'*.

Bibliography

Scripture taken from the HOLY BIBLE, NEW INTERNATIONAL VERSION Copyright 1973, 1978, 1984 International Bible Society. Used by permission of Zondervan Bible Publishers.

1 Corinthians 15:55. The Thompson Chain-Reference Bible. New International Version. Copyright 1990 by The B. B. Kirkbride Bible Company, Inc. The Holy Bible, New International Version. Copyright 1973, 1978. 1984 by International Bible Society. Zondervan Bible Publishers. B. B. Kirkbride Bible Co. Inc. Indianapolis, Indiana, 46204, U. S. A.

Luke 12:31. The Thompson Chain-Reference Bible. New International Version. Copyright 1990 by The B. B. Kirkbride Bible Company, Inc. The Holy Bible, New International Version. Copyright 1973, 1978. 1984 by International Bible Society. Zondervan Bible Publishers. B. B. Kirkbride Bible Co. Inc. Indianapolis, Indiana, 46204, U. S. A.

Matthew 5:16. The Thompson Chain-Reference Bible. New International Version. Copyright 1990 by The B. B. Kirkbride

Bible Company, Inc. The Holy Bible, New International Version. Copyright 1973, 1978. 1984 by International Bible Society. Zondervan Bible Publishers. B. B. Kirkbride Bible Co. Inc. Indianapolis, Indiana, 46204, U. S. A.

Matthew 11:29. The Thompson Chain-Reference Bible. New International Version. Copyright 1990 by The B. B. Kirkbride Bible Company, Inc. The Holy Bible, New International Version. Copyright 1973, 1978. 1984 by International Bible Society. Zondervan Bible Publishers. B. B. Kirkbride Bible Co. Inc. Indianapolis, Indiana, 46204, U. S. A.

Matthew 13:45. The Thompson Chain-Reference Bible. New International Version. Copyright 1990 by The B. B. Kirkbride Bible Company, Inc. The Holy Bible, New International Version. Copyright 1973, 1978. 1984 by International Bible Society. Zondervan Bible Publishers. B. B. Kirkbride Bible Co. Inc. Indianapolis, Indiana, 46204, U. S. A.

Revelation 12:21. The Thompson Chain-Reference Bible. New International Version. Copyright 1990 by The B. B. Kirkbride Bible Company, Inc. The Holy Bible, New International Version. Copyright 1973, 1978. 1984 by International Bible Society. Zondervan Bible Publishers. B. B. Kirkbride Bible Co. Inc. Indianapolis, Indiana, 46204, U. S. A.

Revelation 21. The Thompson Chain-Reference Bible. New International Version. Copyright 1990 by The B. B. Kirkbride Bible Company, Inc. The Holy Bible, New International Version. Copyright 1973, 1978. 1984 by International Bible

Society. Zondervan Bible Publishers. B. B. Kirkbride Bible Co. Inc. Indianapolis, Indiana, 46204, U. S. A.

Song of Solomon. The Thompson Chain-Reference Bible. New International Version. Copyright 1990 by The B. B. Kirkbride Bible Company, Inc. The Holy Bible, New International Version. Copyright 1973, 1978. 1984 by International Bible Society. Zondervan Bible Publishers. B. B. Kirkbride Bible Co. Inc. Indianapolis, Indiana, 46204, U. S. A.

Song of Solomon 2:13. The Thompson Chain-Reference Bible. New International Version. Copyright 1990 by The B. B. Kirkbride Bible Company, Inc. The Holy Bible, New International Version. Copyright 1973, 1978. 1984 by International Bible Society. Zondervan Bible Publishers. B. B. Kirkbride Bible Co. Inc. Indianapolis, Indiana, 46204, U. S. A.

SONGS

More Than Anything. Natalie Grant, 2015. On the Album 'Be One'. Released by Curb Records, 13/11/2015.
I Surrender All. Judson W. Van DeVenter (1855–1939). Put to music by Winfield S. Weeden, 1896.

www.ingramcontent.com/pod-product-compliance
Lightning Source LLC
Chambersburg PA
CBHW062051280525
27284CB00047B/1174